W9-DFD-011

The absorbing personal story of the most dynamic leader of the Black Revolution. It is a testament of great emotional power from which every American can learn much. But, above all, this book shows the Malcolm X that very few people knew, the man behind the stereotyped image of the hate-preacher—a sensitive, proud, highly intelligent man whose plan to move into the mainstream of the Black Revolution was cut short by a hail of assassins' bullets, a man who felt certain he would not live long enough to see this book appear.

"In the agony of [his] self-creation [is] the agony of an entire people in their search for identity. No man has better expressed his people's trapped anguish."

—*The New York Review of Books*